# Fire Flak

A Book of Poetry

By Mark Acraman

I dedicate this collection of poems to my friends, who without, I would not be here.

## On Care Road

Do not let the silence fool you,
The screams are stifled, through and through.

The gentle glint is in their eyes,
Soft smiles grin in wild surprise,
Though the man pretends to sleep,
He hears the words and faintly weeps.

When you walk in the empty hall,
There's no jubilant footfall,
Of yesteryears' purple vigour,
Just vibrant souls that you ignore.

Do not let the silence fool you,
The screams are stifled through.
Do not let the silence pacify,
There is no rest, waiting to die.

## Evergreen- Bitter Scented Oakland Dream

Old rings grow great
But the circles are less perfect.

Have to squint
To make the shape
Stand Stout.

Purple on black-
Looks bright!
Cocaine on weed;
High as a kite.

Some mornings
Stay stale
As old cheese in the fridge.

Stagnant.

No matter how hard I stare,
Or how much I squint,
I can't make the blood
On palace walls
Look like liquorish.

I can't make the holes
In my shirt
Look like buttonholes...
Find the perfect partner-
My hand in hand;
To lead me across this ravished land.

To make it feel alright.
Like human means human.

## 7 Days of Decadence

Woke up,
Had existential crisis,
Went home to bed.

Woke up,
Held hope in my hands,
Had existential crisis,
Went home to bed.

Woke up,
Held hope in my hands,
Saw God tread on an Ant,
Had existential crisis,
Went home to bed.

Woke up,
Tried to be better,
Held hope in my hands,
Saw God tread on an Ant,
Had existential crisis,
Went home to bed.

Woke up,

Saw God tread on an Ant,
Tried to be better,
Became a victim of my own humanity,
Held hope in my hands,
Had existential crisis,
Went home to bed.

Woke up,
Watched the sun rise,
Saw God tread on an Ant,
Tried to be better,
Held hope in my hands,
Became a victim of my own humanity,
Had existential crisis,
Went home to bed.

Woke up,
Saw God tread on an Ant,
Succumbed to darkness,
Tried to be better,
Became a victim of my own humanity,
Held hope in my hands,
Had existential crisis,
Watched the sun rise,
Went home to bed.

## Fire Flakes

Should I compare thee to a summer's day?
So many of my favourite days sway
To dismal states of entropy – deepest
Haze, I float like a red bloated carcass.
Fire burned this skin, curdles- shudders at warmth,
Keep in the shade; degenerate up north,
Spark a conversation- spark elation,
Medusa- overwhelming sensation.
Modest and calm countenance- Athena.
Fierce, warrior clad spirit- Dianna.
Sweet, elegant ethos glides on the wind,
One last nice thought before I am skinned.
Raining down in swarms of crimson raging
Flares- burn permafrost like Hades- Hell- fire.

## Sobriety

Well done,
Just like everyone,
I have my
Uniform,
My clean shirt,
My clean mind.

Getting older now,
Cold,
When lonely-
Stay clean!
Build a future
I never thought I would see.

Step back,
Step forward,
But moved,
Always moved,
Though stagnant-
Not sterile.

Focus!
Don't drift to decay,
Stay!
In the room,
Now,
No psychosis!

# Dear Michael

Faded as that 90's graffiti on the train station walls,
Old locomotives, their engines cease to spin and sputter.
Little mice, too famished in their task, caress cogs and messages,
From places, too dark to read, the notes pile up.
Some, I think, may be blank.
Some, I could not read, as I scribbled those promises too fast.
A great mound of empty words made from a tree now dead.
The cogs move no more, I doubt they were ever connected before…


In line for a one-way ticket out of this grave land,
My baggage gripped tight with both hands- makes it difficult to keep in check,
I try to hide it with a smile, no one offers to help.
Surprisingly sullen, my every movement seems to echo from bold, cold walls,
The insignia behind the ticket master's house is sprayed in red and it reads:
'This was always a one-way trip'
I bite my lip, try to understand how to turn menace into sand,
This station is run by ghosts. I can feel them watching from holes in the wall.

I was asked by a stranger, "why did you come here",
My staggered recoil from justice and reason must have been enough,
When I looked back, my persecutor was lost to an empty hall,
And the bones of this room can be seen when it breathes,
So clear, not seen the sun shine in a long time,
Startled like a bird falling into a pool, I wonder why I came here at all.


I talk to the ticket officer, this hat worn low, talking from a dark place,
I want to know, "the time of the next train please",
But the man only holds my gaze, from beneath his low cap
Motionless, the spindly man holds all the cards, then blows away into the wind.
Left his own station in search of tracks. Somewhere remote
The sun is shining, and life is dead upon this new day.


Perhaps it is too early, I sit and wait for someone to talk to,
"You know that bag must be awfully heavy, please let me carry it for you",

I shake my head and grip what is mine a little tighter,
"Don't be afraid to let me in, I only want to help you free your light",
But I don't care for skin or bones, I set down my bag and watch,
The man of bones, with dreams larger than his stake,
Perhaps, if you were not so far away, you would have the strength to exist,
I look up to see the man who tried so frugally,
Met by dead air, perfectly comfortable- without a friend in the world.


I take a stroll down the decrepit tracks, cold air grasps at skin and sense,
Just to see the colour of the rust, and what the reaction was,
The trains and tracks are turning bitter-brown and discoloured purple,
Holes are manifesting themselves into the carriage, much less comfortable than I ever knew.
I step on the dead cartridge, much less comfortable than I ever-
Reliving a time when the carriage was bright, and laughter echoed the halls,
Far down the musky, dark-grey scope, I can hear the faint sobs of a child,
Inevitably, I find the kid, small and frail, sobbing into his hands from under his hat.

"Dear Michael, this carcass is the last place that I expected to find you",
I kneel down beside the boy and tell him what comes from inside"
"You didn't spend much time here when we were alive, I am leaving you Michael, your world is cold and dead".
The boy trembles before sobbing turns to cold laughter,
He lifts his head and I peer into two dark and empty sockets,
Pristine, white bones contrast the encroaching darkness,
Michael tells me: "There is no leaving this place".


The skeleton child's words are empty.


A little while down the track, darkness pours from every crack,
Each train looks as dead as the one that was mine,
I follow a trail of disfunction to the end of the line,
Where I find a train, most unlike the rest, its silky black skin has been kept intact,
Monstrous, foreboding and intimidating, the conductor keeps the fire stoked,
Red mist puffs from the window, horror stagnant beauty feels and flows.

The walls of the carriage are meticulously decorated,
Framed pictures resting on crimson silk, a life frozen in time,
I am not welcome here,
Presently, a feral scream from far away- the engine room,
A mad man armed with fire eyed fury,
Jackal Rushes through moment and memory in fear and panic,
The first thing in this nightmare clad in skin,
The man stands still, full height, coloured in… I look into his eyes:


I fall back through twisted carriages.
Light.
Butterflies protecting fire from rain.
I sleep safe knowing that no one thinks of me.

## Alcohol (The Liquor Always Wins)

Sweet and supple golden nectar,
Caress my lips, gentle as a kiss,
There is no distance I would not venture,
Nor no succulent sip that I would miss.

The cold perspiration sits on my glass
As the most beautiful woman waiting,
Whisper melody like hypnotic brass
Ensemble, heavenly mood creating.

As you pour yourself down my open throat,
I float in an ocean, calm and serene,
Comfort envelops, warmer than my coat.
You are my only and forever Queen.

Peering through cloudy eyes on the bathroom floor,
The vomit in my throat lets me know I am yours.

# If You Knew...

If you knew
That you were already
Dead,
Would you still go to work?

## Juniper Berries

I am anxious to look or to caress
A beautiful, blooming, illustrious
Vixen. Vibrant; sumptuous red flower,
I would steal your time if just for an hour.
I swing between clovers, petals shelter
Forever. Woodlands help her. Athena:
Towering stature- plethora- no measure.
Tiny spots, flicking hair, untamed treasure.
Beneath inconsequential ethereal
Is something smaller, a single blue thrill-
Charging through empty halls at solid walls.
But the Devil smiles when an Angel falls.

## Lake Windermere

In case you forget,
In all your darkest moments,
Warmth,
Sunshine dancing petulantly on the water.
I would like to share the majesty-
Windermere.

Endless lawns of forlorn, scraggly grass
Stretches and etches hills into life.
Formed from the hand of an artist,
Stroking the countenance
And beaming beauty into its many folds,

Little hovels of black, vert and emerald
Hide like mice and voles,
Shivering in the sanctity
And uncertain security
That the upside-down mounds afford.

The lane is a wash of blue,
Smiling delicately at a distance
Flowing as it waves,
Languid and gay,
Comfortable in it's age.

Island.
But one tree,

Standing helplessly,
Hopelessly, out of place.
Feeling content, in its lovely face.

Even the sky agrees,
For there is no quarrel
Between it and the translucent, ethereal colours
Flooding the canvas.
What is the work of man compared to God?

And how much more beautiful it is than anything I have seen

## Hi! Hail Mary, Lord of all that is Black

I guess it is a relief to see you
Again, my old friend. Cloaked, your head of blue,
You wander among the graves like fireflies,
Absolute darkness, jittering night skies.
It never seems to fail to startle my
Child-like sensation of life passing by.
Orderly rows, rigid cartridge paper,
Ink and tax reports, functions to cater.
Misanthropic, naïve, idealistic
Degenerative and narcissistic,
Paranoid, poisonous, parasitic
Fear giver. Fear receiver. Entropic
Skeleton, dancing in caustic acid,
Looking on. A quiet, forlorn Aphid.

## Red

Red. Blue. Green balloons skip from hand to air.
Their buoyance pulling taught on string without a care
For cutting of birthday cake or pink frosty icing melting
In the sun, party plates pass from Nanna to Papa.
The sleek magic man pulls another trick, waves his hands and 'ta-da'.

The birthday boy sits unblinking,
Whilst those around make merry clinking,
Stupor with drinking.
Unmoved in his party of one.

Pink candy, fluffy pillows, sugar spun round like may pole in June
Sun, gliding through shrouds of baby blue glue on the day when somebody loved you,
The faded scent of burning popcorn scars memory.
Faint, old, warm voices rise in chorus of lukewarm water, embrace the scene
As children in play, chase white rabbits through hedges all summer day.

The birthday boy sits with guard folded,

and his mind is moulded,
his memory of play is shrouded,
thoughts making merry grounded,
unmoved in his party of one.

Sweet, suckling, pig aroma, dancing through the air and making merry
all the guests, with hustle and bustle, meeting and greeting with every
burst of laughter, rising and drowning in the air like Ariel,
Enchantress of Garden chairs, thin napkins caped in Tomato,
Children bounce around on castles, kings clinging to memories of tomorrow

The birthday boy sits far away,
Where his thoughts are free to flay,
All memory of that savage day,
Where innocence and virtue lay,
Unmoved in his party of one,

Ice cream Sundaes glitter as diamonds, yawning and smiling
As cream floats down the exquisite vase in timing
To lecherous looks promising requiem to appetite,
A chorus of laughter fills the air with, pop- another bottle,
Warm embrace of familiar friends, we smile soft as a bubble…

The birthday boy,
with stern and solemn stare,
Dares not cut the air,
Or insist on what is fair,
But sits to fester in the sun's cold glare,
Looking like he does not care,
Unmoved in his party of one.

Sun flakes leaping over my neighbour's
Stubbly white palace, beams trickle round its walls in party favours,
Death lightning blinding, level-climbing, stupor rising, smiling clowns,
Gracefully rummage through pockets for silver-shining keys,
Embraces kind faces with kinder eyes and another cherished memory leaves.

The birthday boy sat silent as the grave,
His parents want him to behave,
No boy like fancies left to save,
Stooped low in his plastic cave,
Ruing the knife that thought him brave.
Unmoved in his party of one.

## 'I Love You'- A Poem by Dementia

Pupils gaze into the sun, I am stunned,
Unearth the power of Raa in your eyes,
Revel! As we lay for long hours, sunned
To death in the warm embrace of your fires.

As we wrap our lives around each other's
Souls as stinging nettles cradle soft skin,
Our life embers trickle, rumbles, smothers-
*Nothing. Just- blood. Scars, filth under cover.*
And you tickle the hair under my chin...

Time swells and the kind universe cradles-
*I can't- stomach this fucking orange juice anymore!*
*I choke on the bits, I told you before,*
*How many times- and where is that whore?*
*What do you mean- "Lucy has gone before"*
*Good Lord, where has that bitch gone now. That whore-*
Cotton wrapped 'round faithful fairy fables —
**Grandad? Is that you? What did you send me for?**

This dream bred a silk no spider could weave,
Heavenly nirvana, none could conceive...

*You. Child like, notions of freedom. So naive,*
*Your fucked up little attitude is hard to conceive.*

**Lucy? Lucy, is that you?** -*You prick tease!*
*I am confused, did you drug me again?-*
I shall follow wherever you may lead...

*-You're no better than when you're on your knees-*
**Don't leave me, like a little frightened Fen...**
Just ask and I should spend my life on my knees.

My light is yours to – blank –

*Tie the rope to the tree and fucking hang.*

**Lucy must be with Grandad, that's why I
Can't find them- can't find my love- my bee.**

How long until this moment passes by
Lucy, do me the Honour. Marry me.

**Lucy?**

Lucy.

# I Don't Remember Your Name

A desperate, bourgeois experience,
Warm red light sneaks through the flimsy curtain
With briefcase and notes, no interference
From reason or conscience, not too certain
About scaling the walls of nihilism
And entering the warm head of dead-space,
Expanding my languid realism,
Rushing the end like a three legged race.
In the dying ashes of apathy
I accidentally caught a glimpse:
Dark and degenerated, flayed clarity,
Depravity... Empathy... Caustic rinse,
To the bone, the skeleton is not white,
I relate most to women of the night.

# I Once Caught a Sparrow

I once caught a sparrow, small and black, its wings shivered as I took it in,
Fed the poor little thing, stroked its breast and listened for a heartbeat,
There it was, small but strong, its pulse erratic. Scared creature,
After the day, it had recovered and was ready to fly away, as it was born to do
So, I broke my sparrow's wings.

Now my sparrow sits in its box, its heart is small and strong,
But I don't let it out to see the light of day for too long,
I love my sparrow, I look at it night and day,
My warm embrace, from time to time, reminds the thing that it's mine,
I keep my sparrow in the dark

Today, my sparrow was looking as effervescent and as strong as ever,
It hopped with pride and glee and looked so lovingly at me,
So, I took it out of its box and placed it by the open window,
The wild-eyed adoration of Raa was in its eyes as it peeped at freedom,

So, I broke my sparrows wings.

My sparrow is looking a little tired and upset,
I placed it in the box without a friend or a strand of hope to live on,
I told my sparrow that I love it and that it is special,
And it believes that I love it as it loves me, but I only like it because it is black.
I keep my sparrow in the dark.

## Time Swells

Time is not a line nor a road,
It doesn't pass by in equal integers:
It grows,
Swells,
Accumulates-
In small moments,
Gets caught in the reefs.
larger pools for more prominent moments.
Boundless depth in a singularity.

To see through the eyes of a dead man,
In a moment long past,
Forget the small,
Happy,
Tranquil,
Streams.
Waves career from the bigger ones,
Crashing into my small boat.

To be cast from the hull
And sink in the singularity,
Be consumed,
Drown.

A moment doesn't pass,
It clings,
Accumulates.

Swipe at the water,
Seeping in,
Try and throw it out,
Before another wave…

The time we spent
Continues to consume,
It swells,
And dwells
In the foreground,
Always.
Time does not pass by,
It is here,
Screaming,
Just as it always has been,
Growing.
Haunting.

I don't think that I can bare
To accumulate anymore of our time.
My lungs are full,
I have choked on the untameable mass of the lamenting sea.

## Cancer

Cut through to the left ventricle,

Like hot knife through butter,

Spreads through life,

Like internal bleeding.

Open hand incision,

Like a drunk surgeon. Having fun.

Burst through the door,

Like riot police.

Get scared,

Like the man hiding squat in the middle.

Chest heaving,

Like the aorta closing.

Wrap my arms around myself,

Like I could stop the world from rocking.

Scream through the crowd at the stage,

Like my words could pierce the veil.

Stand silent under a streetlight,

Like the only light of the world shines

And I am bewildered- dumbfounded; and helpless and hapless.

Like a moth, staring with brevity into the sun until extinguished.

Wide eyed.

Like stepping on a snail.

Digging into supple skin,

Like nails cling to desperate skin

Sinking with the mess we're in.

Like a razor blade,

Held to the edge of your life,

Like playing games with Lucifer,

Who dances to discords of every defeat; every loss of a smile,

Like a wretch-

Writhing in the dark.

Like the smell and taste of dirt

Can't be confined to the ground.


'Like' is a word ready to topple and roll away;

The truth grasps the scruff of your shirt

Like innocent white cotton clings to your heaving lapel;

Holds your hand long after you're in bed.

Like cheap cologne

On a sailor's neck at port.

Like playing-

Alleviates-

Like elevates-

Above the line of filth,

Like a shaky grab-hand trembling under weight,

While your partner looks on in despair,

Like you are fading away

In your fight with misanthropy,

Like a child shouting into a well:

The words come back, but denser,

Like they scabbed over

In the process of burning away…


Like lightning bursting;

Illuminating Magenta sky.

Like the universe creates itself

To fight death,

Like blue flame fights crimson,

Shades begin to run,

Like creating,

A new colour,

Like conjuring,

From air.

Like God.

## Poppies Just Want to Dance

Bouncing bubbles, thin dew stands jubilant
Atop Poppie's vibrant, happy colour.
Poppies in summer time are in a trance,
Smiling rapturously: scarlet music!
C notes rise on a breeze, crimson follows
In a waltz, a samba- zounds, Fiddlesticks!
The garden would be desperately hollow,
Daffodils mope until crimson rhythm
Bursts spontaneous, famous elation
Ricochets, the hanging baskets fathom,
The chain braking freedom born stagnation.
Poppies will dance for the rest of their lives
And drink the sweet nectar, high as a kite.

# The Planets Our Sun Doesn't Shine on

Sunlight pours
On the devout,
Alike, whores.
No moral scout,
A ghost dancing on the moors,
Could just as soon go without.

Morality is a human construct,
The majority of the universe is indifferent to it.

## The 'I' my Clothes Wear Today

I am wearing a dirty shirt,
It is crumpled and twice worn before
On days when laughter echoed the halls
Of aorta and vena cava,
But the sound curdled and went stale
As entropy ran through veins,
As my name rang in your ear,
The animosity grew in your cold stare.


I am wearing odd socks.
I haven't found a partner,
Nor do I understand the use
Of matching two things the same.
If I were in love with the mirror
Then I should just wear one sock,
Let my sock's noose sink into my supple skin
And slowly cut my ankle.


I haven't washed my tie
In the entire time I have owned it,
Or the time it has owned me,
I feel the dirty cotton, wrapped
Tight around my neck-
Binding my words,
Suffocating my suffixes,

And the most heavenly of words have bruises…

The whitest of silken beds,
Was marred with blood
Before it was clad in armour,
Now nothing can harm her.

Nothing gets in..

The covers are not warm
And nobody sleeps there.

Less of a bed now,
Thinks defensively, now.
The colour begins to fade.

Ethereal façade

I don't leave my door open anymore,
Darkness crept in
And I don't dare let it out.
I have grown fond of the colour,
Or lack of it.
Personal pronouns-
The more I use the word 'I',
The less fond I become of it.

**It is Utterly Impossible to Think or Feel More than One Way About a Single Thing, Feeling or Person. Life is Two Dimensional and Astoundingly Simple.**

I still look for you in every room I enter.

I have found myself
Perpetually disappointed.
But only once
Did I find you,
To which I found, myself, reluctant
To talk...

You are still in every room I enter.

The kitchen counter,
The comfy sofa,
My still ruffled and unwashed bed cover.
Like a hammer
Struck to the forefront of my mind,

You are the thing I look for but never hope to find.

## Old Wrath

Wrinkled. Dry faced. Charging down old stairs.
Not what I expected, but I lunged my frantic knife.
Wild eyes turn to wells as aged bright stars stare back.
Heart shattered visage glides, bumbling. Mirage.


Please go do some gardening. Your flowers are
Sick without you. I miss you. Dream spoilt. Crooked,
Half-hearted, direful springs sprout poison youth.
Seedlings blight your wrathful name as petals grow…


The flowers you grew colourless now bloom bright.
They miss grey! True blue is cold- burdened purple.
Feel the life drink backward, clutching an endless
Night you downed tools without final reconcile
Or friend blinded from drugs.
Now staring beyond a time-stained bitter fire,
Burnt images caught and thrust through empty dark
Tortured fear-stricken blood wincing agony- fuck.


Fate lamenting, sharply-flashing, tortured picture,
Lying motionless. Bleeding internally.

## Garden Roses Look Toward the Woodland

Blood-rich, vibrant, swirling petals dance, swing
Around breezes, tremble petulantly,
Feeling power course: green heartfelt stems sing,
Wearing thorn-mail, blazon, nonchalantly.
Cruel thoughts drift timidly toward the wood,
Shady under-shadows conceal pollen,
Ash bees sing the Roses' song- Ruby food
Feeding volcanic hearts, single chronons
Bounce between young cupid's glass heart garden,
Dream half coloured mirage: Wood-Nirvana.
Water drips and sputters, flower haven
Calls from woodlands as Father to Maiden,
Calling gently to sail, meander home.
Rest safe in the halls of horticulture.

## Ballad of Heathcliff/ A Thousand Love Letters for Cathy

I am the tortured, misanthropic ghost

That was tirelessly using your spirit as a host,

Like an oyster, you opened what once was closed

And wander dreamlessly toward the coast

To rest on sea breeze

As I cry, beg and choke on my knees

As Plato in the last moment of Socrates,

Cathy please.

The cold eating at my soul is worse,

As the wind tears at my flesh- furious,

Cathy's ghost walks calmly towards the tempest,

I walk after my heart's crest

With the same colour swirling,

Chaos neatly perpetuating,

I crave the inebriating

Nectar, my centre in the centre of your storm raging.

*Cathy was rapturous and held herself aloft,*

*Heathcliff's heart for Cathy: pillow- soft,*

*Dead to everyone but her- like cloth*

*Covered craggy rocks, like bright, fluttering light to a moth.*

Torcher my soul,

Rain down with the same, unrelenting, cruel

Empathy for a broken fool,

And I'll drown in an ecstasy pool.

*Inseparable branches of an oak tree*

*Wrapped tight around each other's trunk, free*

*From persecution and no none else could see*

"Cathy- you were always perfect to me."

In your breast is where I sleep deepest,

Cradling the poison you cherish and keepest,

Blood thirsty, life-rupturing, reality disintegrating tempest

Ripping out roots in my mind of what I fearest.

Stand and be counted you fearless Hyperion!

Stand against the truth and unrelenting reason

Like a crusader against the heart's treason

You are the ghost and I am the unrelenting daemon!

Covered from crown to heart,

Filled to the summit with desirous art

And shiver, Listening to requiem's Mozart,

To dance in a hall of dirt and claret.

Dancing a waltz on the airy moors,

To keep choking on love's light spoors,

And give into my soul's every amour,

To be crushed under the weight of her every abhor.

I tread on embers of fallen stars

To be burnt with the memory of our long hours,

Trying to fill the space left by Jupiter with Mars

My view of heaven blocked by the chandeliers.

My window is cracked,

Losing that to which long hours lacked,

Following the footfalls back, I tracked

The grave and the words upon it, the character attacked.

To be buried with that lie. Linton,

Before I pulled you from the earth, you moaned so wanton,

Like a frantic beetle struggles on

To drown in water than to be smothered by cotton.

Die in the embrace of one whose arms are like sulphur,

Burning through your form on a

Whim, the bored fancy of a wretch who taught her

Life is not worth living after a daughter.

*An excellent husband of excellent breed,*

*Linton's wealth was enough to feed,*

*All of Cathy's wealthy desires and needs,*

*While Heathcliff's heart was left to bleed.*

We shall live on in the eternity of our last moment,

Etched in memory, forever, like a bronzed monument

That melts, but to the sun's amazement,

The change in state could not change our merriment.
/ could not close our garden's gate


Cathy, I have walked in sleepless dreams,

Limbo, Chasing your ghost. It teems

Inside of me, your spirit glows and gleams.

We are the same character, operating on different themes.

I can't live without my heart,

You are nothing but wonder and art,

I am but bones and claret.

I don't want to live this world if you are not a part.

I can't live without my soul,

The best part of me will die; I will no longer be whole,

To have and to hold in this mortal parole,


All the angels in heaven and still they cannot console.


*Catherine's daughter was born that evening,*

*And the moss covering the grave has started greening.*

*And Cathy was borne that evening,*

*The moss covering the grave is still greening.*

Haunt me Cathy!

I have believed in spirits always,

Don't you dare leave me here and go away!

I am an actor to be used in your play.

I must see you!

The sky is no longer blue.

I can sense your presence, but I look straight through

The ethereal, translucent mourning dew.

I dig with ferocity at your grave to find,

You were much closer than I had in mind,

Because as the hands of the clock unwind,

My heart to beat, I must remind.

"Take any form, drive me mad".

And I shall take Isabella and add

The torture and unreasoning pain she had,

To give Edgar his due- iron clad.

With Catherine on the edge of my periphery

And watching Cathy grow up, a mystery,

How much like the mother in majesty,

To be smothered by Edgar a tragedy.

\*\*\*\*\*\*\*\*\*\*\*\*\*\*\*\*\*\*\*\*\*\*\*\*\*\*\*\*\*\*\*\*\*\*\*\*\*\*\*\*\*\*\*\*\*\*\*\*\*\*\*\*\*\*\*\*\*\*\*\*\*\*\*\*\*\*\*\*\*\*\*\*\*\*\*\*\*\*

*And Heathcliff was perfect to Cathy,*

*Except for status, love's antipathy,*

*Heathcliff couldn't force bloom from their tree,*

*And Cathy married for money.*

*An excellent husband of excellent breed,*

*Linton's wealth was enough to feed,*

*All of Cathy's wealthy desires and needs,*

*While Heathcliff's heart was left to bleed.*

*Far away Heathcliff ran away,*

*To rise through the ranks of masculinity*

*To play, to study, to decay*

*Or find different ways to be led astray…*

*But stray he did not forever,*

*But into the lioness' den he did enter,*

*With diabolical plan, not clever,*

*But the means to end all ties, to sever…*

*But love grew such wings*

*That though darkness encroaches and sings,*

*His bleeding heart, to love, it clings,*

*A sharp knife to his enemy's house it brings.*

*Upon the meeting, eyes glistening,*

*Old love had not stopped singing,*

*Neither had stopped listening,*

*And to Edgar's heart- a wretched clenching.*

Edgar you learn'ed fool,

Weak bodied, my enemy, cruel,

Vile, keeper of the only beautiful

Free bird alive, chained at the neck with manacle…

Though free now form her mortal chain,

She can be with me always, my neck I crane

To see her, but I can't see, it's all the same

Ethereal terrain.

*Edgar tried to keep the woman he love'd,*
*But her love for Heathcliff erupted,*
*But her mind, body or soul: he did not corrupt,*
*Just try to keep the woman he loved.*

Poor little Cathy, you deserve so much better,
So, in my son's hand I wrote a letter,
My love was raging even inside her daughter,
She could not resist and I caught her.
Locked her up and turned the key upon her fast,
So I knew her marriage to my son would last,
My net to Wuthering heights is cast,
Such humble beginnings- such contrast.

*A wicked woman with a baby inside,*
*Only love for Heathcliff inside,*
*But couldn't stem the tide.*
*Cathy and Heathcliff- In one heart reside.*

I can hear your voice catching on the wind,

Calling me- I am far behind,

But nearer now than ever in my mind,

Caring callously, profusely for what I find.

Can you? Cathy! Cathy! Cathy! Please release me,

From the mortal coil story,

Extract your catharticism, set me free

From this translucent tyranny.

*You groan in a broken dream,*

*Stumbling to feel out the seam*

*Of the echo of Cathy's eye-gleam,*

*Torn apart without the better half of your team.*

*Once upon time, Heathcliff was picked up from the street,*

*Or was it an affair, another woman Daddy did sleep,*

*But kept you safe, his promise he did keep,*

*Rolling in filth, knee deep.*

*Cathy couldn't keep her hands from the young man,*

*Kindred souls from minute one, hand- in- hand,*

*But the rest of the family, his face they could not stand,*

*So they played on the moors, the surrounding lands.*

*Forever.*

Forever

## Night like Day

Slithers of light trickle through cracks in the day,

Find a million variations, a million ways to say,

"What use is there in saying",

Grief accumulated over time, now I am paying- for what's

Far down the crevasse, screams shrouded and muffled

Come from far further than i had ever expected...

A pack of wounded cards are shuffled

And dealt with ferocity, like they were infected

There are things in that darkness that I never meant to lose:

The glitter on my day and the ability to listen to the blues,

The warmth within my heart, i thought a monkey on my back,

I kind of miss the people that would call me a twat.

To violence and war, I frivolously tossed aside

Instead of being swallowed up in the pain of the day.

I wish to tell you a secret, please let me confide

I wish I had stayed and died in the ruin and decay.

For the disclosure of the bright and cheery darkness, there is a price to pay,

The speckled flakes of youth and innocence break away like dry clay

Scattered to the wind, floating on waves of melody

Made by broken homeless loveless men, hanging words out like laundry,

Crushing leaves underfoot with placid brows,

To dissuade mechanical minds from manacles mentally made,

While above, many work together to spread messages of hate in the clouds-

Cold minded monsters can kill me and scrub at the words but they won't fade!

The words hang in the air, find a way

In their dance, absorbing light and putting it to work on play,

Twist the already deformed nature of progress

To make it run backward and prey will eat the lioness,

Empty halls, full to the brim by zombie,

Dead beyond the eyes, shattered hearts make shattered dreams,

But if I can just bring people to life then maybe

We can change culture, make it warmer than it seems

Faning the same kind of love and security

That your eyes seem to bleed through immaturity

If I can lead you to a better fate then maybe I can find redemption,

Find something decent inside of being smothered by narcissism.

## Cheering up the Daffodils

Happy, drooping, yellow blossom over-
Hangs and peers drearily toward the dirt.
Leering with might, towering poor clover
Who trembles and asks, "How was one so hurt?"

Daffodil smiles a wry smile and chuckles,
"Young one, the tides of time meander, break,
Thrash the fearful boat until it buckles,
Naivety led me to this glum state".

Clover sat in quiet contemplation
Until, "Daffodil, you are a victim
Of turning time's sad manipulation,
Revere the present- make it your kingdom.

Startled, the proud, tall flower spoke no words,
Craned neck to the sun, drank plentifully.
At length, listened to the sound of the birds,
Saw beauty in the garden, presently.

"Colour, the wealth enriching this garden
Feels to me, a small boat in the ocean
Beating on against the tide- a burden,
An ill-fated, cumbersome devotion".

A blue Jay sensed the trouble from the trees,
Made a detour from its usual way,
Beseeched the flower, hopped down to her knees,
"Not everything in this world fades to grey.

This life can be free and beautiful, Daf!
Grow so tall but you rarely see the sky,
Take a look in the endless blue and laugh,
The bright yellow orb will never need die".

Languid flower feels the sun on his neck,
The rays passing through his delicate hands,
He cranes his head toward the ground to check
The answer does not lie in the brown lands.

Eyes as feelers pointed toward the ground,
A wriggling worm wraps around the words,
"Dear flower, you make a terrible sound,
Being so down, I have come to be heard.

The dirt that nourishes you so freely
Has God's plan in every grain of soil,
The world is connected in every
Facet, in every beautiful smile".

We are your friends, the life that cares for you,
So if you can't be alive for yourself,
If you can't find a reason to live too,
Keep spreading magic for your friends, get through.

# Stroke of Death

Forlorn,
I sit and mourn
What could have been,
From the boundary, trying not to be seen.

Misanthropic.
A tiny nick
Has snuffed out my life,
Success always resting on the edge of a knife.

Melancholy,
I sit here pondering, sorry.
Should be out there fighting.
Every strike sounding like lighting.

Company,
I rushed too hurriedly,
Spurned our honour
And became cannon fodder,

Because I got the plan wrong,
Sung the wrong song,
Overstretched,
Regret etched

Across my face,
Death dressed in lace,

Struggling on a sticky wicket,
I guess that is just cricket.

## Maze Mouse

The first time
I lost my mind,
The world seemed a destitute place.

The first time
I took it by force.
Left to fend with fiends

Furrowing through time,
Clawing at the day,
Dragging myself against the pull.

Life,
The introduction to
Something dark and true.

The second time!
I could stand no more
Of what I found before

Did not mean to come back,
Sometimes I think I didn't,
Mulling in a mood grey and grave

The blue sky,
Once bubbly
Now looks blander

Circle of red.

Head of lead.
Lying in my bed.

The third
barely touched
Just scraped at chalk.

After that, I went away…
Opted out.
Nothing mattered.

There I sat in limbo.
Soured.
Dissasociated

Like an old car,
I sputtered,
Bore sitting and rusting.

Consumed.
Floating
Dead-eyed.

And how I laugh,
To say
That I am less

How I laugh-
To say that I am dying
To think that I am sloth

Sloth?

I am greed.
I am pride.

I am failure,
I am afraid-
Of everything.

I died some time ago,
Left company
Alone

So now I am back in the game.
And enigmatic.
Do I scare you?

Because I should.
I am terrifying
And can't be intimidated

I do not fear death,
I do not fear reprobation
But honestly?

I scare my self
And I am afraid of you too,
Fear is my super power.

Depression is my identity,
Something personal to me,
So-

So Welcome death,

Welcome fear!
Welcome Might.

You can't comprehend me,
What it is to be free,
You have never died

Never writhed,
In fire,
You circuit.

I shan't come out tonight,
Or any other
Night

But stand afront,
With twisted mind, bald and blunt
And I shall eat you…

That look-
Look down
Disgust

Divert your eyes,
But stand in my way,
And I shall eat you

Your eyes-
Coal,
Fresh grass

Red light

Yellow filter
Green eyes

Pain defies
Lies
Anguish flies

Panic stricken,
Anxiety driven
Rapture.

Quick- Look down now,
Holding back the wrath of Jessu,
This mouse will fucking eat you!

# Dear journal

I- have hurt myself; again.

Cut my mind on idealism.

Bled marked pragmatism,

Cried an empty nihilism

Bound,

Air waves wrap tight around bloody,

Wrists, the red soaked skin absorbs noisy

Poison, flows crimson,

Strays darker…

Stoke the fire,

Coal is black,

Death has come,

Knocking at your..

I feel choked.

Perpetuating humanity,

The single nature of love and care,

While just out there I ruffled your hair.

Proof of unison,

Un je forme

Fall to the floor in ashes,

One carriage, a closed journey.

With wonderfully bright plastic views,

Try, to fool my filter to believe,

These plastic truths.

May I take a photograph?

And pray that someone finds me.

# Looming

Why now? "Don't look through the ancient window",

"You seek to march, but follow orders- hold!"

I fall back, holding my position, black crow-

Furrowing malice through my mind, snow- cold.

Head down, trench deep fanatic death wonder,

Crossing crimson lines, fate unwinds, touch- spark,

Breath curdles in my ear like old thunder,

Sleep paralysis, fraught small child at heart.

The dark smeared scorn feeds on my sun drenched form.

## Where Water Lilies Sleep

Far beyond the tall and snowy mountains,
Lies a place where men and women can dream
Wholesome, they fall in love by the fountains
And with passion, their eyes glisten and gleam.

Oh dream, dream, dream where water lilies sleep,
Oh dream, dream, dream where water lilies sleep

Where the waters whisper secrets of life,
The two suns are reflected in our eyes,
By the verge, I would ask you to my wife
And together we could live in the skies.

Oh dream, dream, dream where water lilies sleep,
Oh dream, dream, dream where water lilies sleep

To my love, heavenly matrimony,
Forever, as sweet as nectar in my ears,
Adoration could last eternity

And set ablaze to all our earthly fears.

Oh dream, dream, dream where water lilies sleep,
Oh dream, dream, dream where water lilies sleep,
Tell me all your secrets and I shall keep
Them with me, as the people of earth weep.

And now we are one and everlasting,
There is no one that can keep us apart,
The two suns are forever contrasting,
I shall live underwater with my heart.

Oh dream, dream, dream where water lilies sleep,
Oh dream, dream, dream where water lilies sleep.

## Absurd Reality

Blackbirds sit motionless, melancholy.
Feathers pure as a cast iron cauldron,
Their spell ceased now and frozen timelessly.
Never alive, witness the dead squadron.

No blood raging through veins long since dried up,
Long legs appear sprung, yet time moves not, Broken-
Passage, nothing remains to interrupt,
A thousand words of wisdom unspoken....

Misanthropic wings flutter all at once!
Jubilant howls of vigour, rise chorus
Of melody, serene, enchanting flux,
Time flies through darkness, perpetually porous.

Fear stricken agony stills the pretty mind.
We find new colours than those we were assigned.

# The Dying Embers

It breaks my heart to hear myself talk so distantly,
Of trivial and jovial and boyish nonsense.
It breaks my heart to hear you talk so rapturously,
Of desire and passion-lusting, covetous and obsessive sex.
We both know that we talk in safe houses
To avoid the abrasive fact.
We are avoiding talking of love;
That would break our heart.

## Sing Us One Last Song You Mess

The remnants of my intelligence and dignity,
John can take to his grave,
I just wanted to fight, for what was right
But was swallowed in a wave of reality.
I once tried to hold out idealism,
To have it smashed in a thousand pieces,
I thought that people should care for each other,
To be told it wasn't economically viable.

To another best friend that never really cared,
I loved you more than you will ever know,
You were one of the hardest people I ever let go,
But you used me and abused me just like everyone else,
Pretended to care and dictated fair,
I was blinded by delirium,
And could not see, that the beautiful trees,
Were plastic, lifeless and cold.

The music is beginning to sound like silence,
I keep getting the melody stuck in my head,
I forgot how it began and can't see past
The first verse, but I know the album artwork:
A man in a hearse- the picture looks familiar,
I feel like I was there, somewhere, floating through

air,
The beat is inconsistent and I can't find anything I like,
It just passes right through me.

The field where we buried Pete's ashes,
Will be forever green to me,
It glows with his smile and snowy white hair,
But no one remembers he's there!
And those that do pass over the spot without a care,
But the light of the world seems darker
Without his wonderful wintery hair.
When you laughed, I laughed and when you smiled- I felt safe.

Of course, to you- my love, the ever lingering
Hopeful lady of my earth. My feelings were always true,
I longed for you with depth of colour unknown,
To any time or place I would have flown,
But just like you said,
You were incapable of love- nothing but spite,
You pulled out my brittle heart out and fucked it.
You hurt me more than I hurt myself.

And how- I hurt myself- delved into a rabbit hole,
That I was too young to be thrust down,
I cut my mind on razor sharp thoughts:
Potential- and felt like a failure.
I could not sleep for the longest time, I was kept awake

By a tear-soaked pillow that reeked with the fumes of alcohol,
I would lay awake all night long
And scold me for being too stupid.

The smallest of spotted and winged bugs,
Can't set foot on the cusp of my shoelace,
The keenest eyed falcon, misses the outline of fragility,
Cold and stagnant sensation, carried on the wind,
Does not reach my eyes,
Or make the duct empty,
Roaring shrieks run through my ears,
Cowering or apathetic eyes can't set fire to these fears.

I am so sorry to the smallest of you winged creatures,
You won't understand- probably ever,
But know that I never meant to cause you pain,
You look at the world through such a small scope,
Please don't ask me how I struggle to cope,
You are one of the reasons I fought the dark for so long,
To start out- you looked at me and I thought you would understand,
But you turned out uniform- blind and deaf and dumb.

I can't tell you the depth of these memories,
In the garden, where a voice spoke to me so smooth,
And sweet and petals and aroma seemed to float
On breezes heralded with happy sparks, buoyant

Through seas of troubles, until those troubles dock
In a harbour that I wrecked, degrading in grief,
Sweet flowers have been rotting in time and now
The words that were music are now virus, reckoning
every moment.

My brother refuses to wear his glasses now,
He says he can't see anything clearly anymore,
For the tears won't tear themselves away
From the rocky, half dead, sunken terrain, sees
The light of day less often than flesh eating worms,
Sharp teeth grin and the rose-coloured memory
Of playing football in the park after dark,
Or cricket on the old wicket- I hope you miss me the
most- I would you.

I flew to my mother's house,
But she wasn't home; I let myself in,
Looked over the empty wine bottles,
Stacked in pairs, so they each have a friend.
The pictures on the walls are all forty years old,
And the characters are all face down,
I can't pick them up,
The image of agony is plastered to the floor with no
one to adore.

My father's tools are all strewn in the garden,
Plugged in without power- hiding round corners,
they cower,
The shaky lawn mower cried internally,
Because all it could do was cut the bloody grass,

But could not cut the ties of familiarity,
With tiresome fire, turning the content to ashes.
The door to the shed is always a jar,
The boards are flayed and splintered with paint,
dripping to the floor.

Sitting silently in this empty old house,
The creaking of the floorboards seem to know me,
Old memories bounce from hall to wall,
Like an echo of the stagnant fury, that reverberated
From still wall and whispering grief,
Words of narcissism curl in on themselves,
Fatter and nastier than a thousand-pointed needles
Or razorblades, smiling delicately on cupid's
bathroom floor.

Dragging stains and paints across a happy little
corridor,
Smiling at a pattern of pure undeniable psychopathy,
A vibrant and living testament to a society,
Cruel and frowning, scolding the colour,
It doesn't matter what colour!
The deepest shade of purples melts into
Dried crimson mess congealed and defeated on the
floor,
No deviance from black, white and grey anymore.

My footfall does not make a sound.
Nor does my form disturb the gentle snowflakes.
From falling straight down through the empty air,
No blades of grass twist or move from their

Position of placid translucence.
I feel cold as people walk straight through,
The ethereal outline of my faded countenance.
Shivering shade of something real.

The conversation of the officer at the station:
"I can't say the details of the death were
At any detriment to the case,
He stopped living and fell off the face of the earth,
A simple, open and closed case"
I stare hopelessly through the veil,
As the man put down his phone,
And entered suspended animation.

www.ingramcontent.com/pod-product-compliance
Ingram Content Group UK Ltd.
Pitfield, Milton Keynes, MK11 3LW, UK
UKHW021428160525
5949UKWH00027B/717

9 798864 649466